The Japanese Codes

CW00419079

CONTENTS

The Author
Sue Jarvis was one of the Trustees of the Bletchley Park Trust. She took her BA in
British & European History at Liverpool and her MA in Oriental History at the School
of Oriental and African studies at London

© 1997 Sue Jarvis

1

EVENTS AND NEGOTIATIONS LEADING UP TO PEARL HARBOR

In the early days of this study, I was told that the one question which everyone would want to ask was "Did Churchill know about the attack on Pearl Harbor in advance – and did he withhold this information from the Americans so that they would be forced to enter the war?"

So it seemed logical then to make this subject one of the main topics, since it has a great deal to do with signals intelligence.

But it is necessary first to give some background information, if only because a European view of the war tends to make people forget what was happening in the Far East. Japan had been longer at war than any of the European powers, for she had been engaged in an undeclared war with China since July 1937. It is easy to forget that from 1902 until 1921, Japan and Britain were allies and this alliance was renewed in 1911. It followed Japan's active support for the Western nations when their legations in Peking were besieged during the Boxer Rebellion. During the First World War Japan sent ships to the Mediterranean to protect British convoys. In 1905 Japan defeated Russia in the Russo-Japanese War, and by the Treaty of Portsmouth she acquired the former Russian rights in Manchuria, which was a Chinese territory but the rights had been leased to Russia in 1898. These included mining concessions and the South Manchurian Railway newly built by Russia, together with the right to station an army to protect it. Japan's historic enemy was Russia and she saw this large area as a buffer zone.

In Japan, ideas of their country as a "have-not" nation, lacking the resources to become a truly modern industrial society had become widespread, and she was determined to exploit her Manchurian gains to the full. Japan also received the southern half of Sakhalin (the island north of Japan) and recognition of her "paramount interest" in Korea (which led to its annexation in 1910). The Washington Conference of 1921-22 established peace in the Far East, and by the Five Power Pact agreed the ratio of capital ships between Japan, Britain and the US as 3:5:5. Britain and America would not build fortifications east of Singapore or west of Hawaii. But one of the casualties of this agreement was the Anglo-Japanese Alliance which the US wished Britain to give up in the interests of all powers acting together and preserving Chinese integrity. Many people have speculated whether the continuation of this alliance would have made any difference to the war.

For almost a decade the Washington arrangements kept the peace in the Far East. But with the rise of Chiang Kai-shek during the late 1920s Chinese nationalism had greatly increased and in 1931 the Japanese Army in Manchuria staged an incident as a pretext for overrunning the whole province and protecting Japan's considerable investment in it. In 1932 it was proclaimed the independent state of Manchukuo, under the puppet Emperor Pu Yi, the last of the Qing emperors.

The Lytton Commission was sent in 1932 by the League of Nations to investigate the takeover of Manchuria. Although recognising Japan's special interests, it found that she had been the aggressor and recommended non-recognition of Manchukuo. Japan withdrew from the League but the decision further enraged the extreme nationalists in the Japanese Army. Some of these who were mainly younger officers, belonged to secret societies who carried out a number of "patriotic" assassinations of politicians whose views were less belligerent than their own. This inevitably pushed the government to the right, since there was a good deal of public support for the Army's actions. The Army and Navy in Japan had a disproportionate influence on politics because their Ministers were directly responsible to the Emperor and not to the elected government. If these Ministers resigned, or were not appointed, a cabinet could be wrecked.

In 1935 at the London Naval Conference Japan insisted on naval parity with the US, and when this was refused, she walked out. In 1936 she joined the Anti-Comintern Pact. War with China started over a trivial incident known as Marco Polo Bridge. Japan was particularly anxious to station troops in N. China as a buffer zone against the large forces the USSR had on that border, but the Chinese felt this was a violation of their sovereignty.

Reduced to their bare essentials the main positions in 1937 – 41 were:-

• The Japanese government expected China to give in and make peace rapidly on her terms. But Chiang Kai-shek withdrew his government to Chongqing in Sichuan (southwest China) and refused to agree to any settlement. This caused the war to escalate, as Japan gradually overran more and more of China's territory, hoping to bring about the desired settlement. But this did not happen. China is a huge country and Japan got bogged down there – it could not defeat and hold down the whole country.

• US policy was to try to get Japan to make peace with China, and withdraw her troops – because she had upset the peaceful arrangements made for China at the Washington Conference in 1921. But the US was not prepared to take positive action at first in support of her policy.

Having signed the Anti-Comintern Pact in 1936, Japan felt betrayed when in August 1939 Germany and the Soviet Union signed the Molotov-Ribbentrop Pact, particularly as Japan was engaged in battles with Russia on the Manchurian/Mongolian border.

When the European war broke out Admiral Yonai's government tried to improve relations with Britain and the US, but the US stuck to its China conditions. Yonai began pressure to station troops in North Indochina, and to get oil from the Dutch East Indies. The US imposed licences to limit export of aviation fuel, steel and scrap iron to Japan. But with Germany's rapid victories in Europe in 1940 Yonai's government fell, and Konoe's cabinet with Matsuoka, its pro-German Foreign Minister, was the most militant yet. The Tripartite Pact between Japan, Germany and Italy was signed in September 1940.

This was the point at which Japan's entry into the European war became a real possibility, and caused British alarm for the safety of Hong Kong and the Far Eastern possessions. Japan hoped that the alliance with Germany would neutralise the Russian threat to Northern China, and that Britain might soon be overrun as the other European countries had been, leaving South-east Asia undefended. Germany also expected benefits from Japan attacking British possessions and diverting forces away from Europe.

Japan's policy was dangerously opportunist, for by April 1941 it was apparent that Hitler's invasion of Britain was not going to happen, and Britain had not collapsed. When in June 1941 Hitler attacked the USSR without warning his ally, Japan was in a vulnerable position again with Russia.

By the beginning of 1941 US/Japanese relations had entered a more confrontational phase. In November 1940 Roosevelt had for the first time authorised financial help to Chiang Kai-shek – the first instalment of enormous subsidies that Chiang was given to keep China in the war. The US continued to impose economic sanctions on materials Japan needed. The US Ambassador in Tokyo, Joseph Grew, had consistently warned that such actions would encourage the Japanese militants and inflame public opinion – which they did. As the Japanese war effort was affected, far from producing any thoughts of peace, Japan began to plan the seizure of alternative sources.

During almost the whole of 1941 during the run-up to Pearl Harbor, both the British and the US governments were able to listen to the diplomatic traffic between Tokyo and her embassies, in Berlin, Rome, Lisbon, Madrid, Stockholm, Istanbul, Ankara, Berne and of course Washington. Between the wars all the main powers had been engaged in decrypting each other's diplomatic traffic wherever they could. The British Government Code & Cypher School had been set up in 1919 and some of its staff had worked on naval and diplomatic traffic during the First World War. The amount of service traffic in peacetime was small, so until the 1939 war started they worked mainly on diplomatic codes. GCCS was a department of the Foreign Office but was the responsibility of Admiral Hugh Sinclair, the Head of SIS – the Secret Intelligence Service – it was not an armed Service organisation. [3] GCCS moved to Bletchley Park in 1938 and continued its diplomatic work, although with the outbreak of war it was the German services traffic that expanded so enormously. Italian and Russian code work also increased.

It is not possible to consider Britain's part in the Far Eastern War, or her codebreaking efforts against Japan, without also considering the United States. Despite the large territories belonging to Britain which were overrun, we were a secondary player in the Far East because our desperate position in the European war made it impossible for us to be anything more. Also, we had been at war in Europe for over two years and alone since the fall of France in June 1940, while in the Pacific War the Americans were there from the start.

The Americans too had listened to the interwar diplomatic traffic. In 1936, *their* SIS – the Signal Intelligence Service of the US Army – had broken RED, the main diplomatic cipher. In 1938 RED revealed that a new cipher machine was under construction, and on 20 March 1939 the first diplomatic messages in the new machine cipher appeared. This machine was called PURPLE by SIS, and over the next three months RED was phased out and replaced by PURPLE. It took 18 months of strenuous effort for the famous cryptanalyst William Friedman and his team at SIS to break the PURPLE code. This was finally achieved on 20 September 1940, at an opportune moment, for only a week later Japan signed the Tripartite Pact and stationed troops in N. Indochina.

MAGIC became the codeword for American intelligence gained by codebreaking (including the PURPLE machine information), as ULTRA was for intelligence gained by codebreaking in Bletchley Park. The name MAGIC came from the US Army's Chief Signals Officer Maj. Gen. Joseph Mauborgne calling the SIS team "magicians" when they broke the PURPLE code. [4]

The US Navy's Naval Code & Signal Section – now called Op-20-G – had actually co-operated for 4 months with SIS in trying to break PURPLE, although they usually worked on Japanese naval codes. Co-operation was unusual because the US Army and Navy were at daggers drawn for most of the time, even during the war. Their rivalry led to a most curious arrangement – once PURPLE had been broken SIS and Op-20-G took turn and turn about with the decryption. The Army received all traffic with even dates, and the Navy all traffic with odd dates, so as to avoid duplication of effort, and so that neither should gain an advantage! [5]

Churchill had always been interested in signals intelligence, not just in summaries of the information given in decrypts, but in seeing the decrypts themselves. He had been involved with decrypts since 1915 when he was First Lord of the Admiralty, and had set up the procedure for dealing with naval decrypts when the Admiralty's Room 40 was established. On 5 August 1940 he ordered a daily selection of original intelligence documents to be submitted to him personally 'in their original form'. [6]

The decrypts submitted to him were called BJ telegrams, or 'blue jackets' because they were in blue covers. [7] In 1993 those dating from 1941-45 started to be released to the Public Record Office, where they are filed under HW1 in the Index system. It is fascinating to see these papers, many initialled "WSC" and some still in their blue jackets.

BRITISH/US INTELLIGENCE CO-OPERATION BEFORE PEARL HARBOR

William Stephenson, the "man called Intrepid", played a considerable part in the early discussions of intelligence co-operation. But when General Strong on 31 August 1940 proposed "a free exchange of intelligence", including Sigint, to the British Chiefs of Staff, the US Navy opposed this though Stimson, the Secretary for War supported it, as did Roosevelt and the Secretary of State Cordell Hull. But at that early time Britain was unwilling to reveal the breaking of the Luftwaffe Enigma code, one of her most closely-guarded secrets, fearing with some justification that US security was not as tight as our own, and because we also decrypted American diplomatic cables!

In the period June 1939 – September 1940 before PURPLE was cracked, GCCS had also lost this main Japanese diplomatic code. However, in February 1941 SIS cryptanalysts delivered a copy of a PURPLE machine to Bletchley Park and explained its workings. Britain provided some intelligence in return, but not of the existence of the Bombes for breaking Enigma codes. [8]

In November 1940 the Germans came into possession of information of the greatest value to Japan. That summer Churchill had asked the Chiefs of Staff to report on the defence of the Far East. Their report stated that Britain could not defend Hong Kong, Malaya, and Singapore if Japan attacked them because Britain could not produce a Far Eastern fleet. It was decided not to send copies of the report to the Australian or New Zealand Governments, just to the C-in-C Far East at Singapore. In September it was sent by courier on board the Blue Funnel Line steamer *Automedon*.
On 11 November 1940 the *Automedon* was intercepted by the German surface raider *Atlantis* in the Indian Ocean and sunk. But she was boarded and searched first; the report was seized. The information reached Hitler from the German Embassy in Tokyo, and he had it passed to the Japanese naval attaché in Berlin. Britain learned of the *Automedon's* sinking, but did not discover until 30 December that the report had been captured. This was a disaster that gave enormous encouragement to the Japanese militarists. [9]

Yet it would be wrong to imagine that no one in Japan was against war with the United States. Admiral Yamamoto had been a student at Harvard, had worked in the USA and knew that Japan could not rival its economic strength. He warned against war many times, but was ordered to plan the attack on Pearl Harbor.

Between February and December 1941, Cordell Hull and the new Japanese Ambassador Admiral Nomura, held negotiations which were supposed to improve US/Japanese relations. Nomura had been sent because he had known Roosevelt since World War 1, but his task was unenviable, if not hopeless, because the Foreign Minister Matsuoka was not prepared to offer any concessions. MAGIC enabled the Americans to learn a good deal about Japan's real aims, as opposed to what Nomura was saying in the negotiations, because he was inclined to tone down each side's statements.

Oshima, the Japanese Ambassador in Berlin was a particularly good source of information, not only at this critical time but at many others (as will be seen later).

In May 1941 a potentially serious problem occurred. MAGIC revealed Oshima's report that he had been warned by an "absolutely reliable source" that the Americans had broken the Japanese diplomatic code. Some MAGIC material, sent from the British Embassy in Washington by error in a code meant for less confidential matters, was probably decrypted by the Germans. Nomura reported to Tokyo that the US was reading some of their codes but he did not know which. Yet the Japanese concluded PURPLE was still a secure system.

In June 1941 Germany invaded Russia. The Japanese government thought this might be a quick campaign like the European ones. But Germany found, as Japan had in China, that she could not subdue such a large country, especially one that resisted so fiercely. In July MAGIC showed Japan's preparations for the occupation of French Indochina. Roosevelt responded by an oil embargo and freezing of Japanese assets in the US. Britain and the Netherlands followed suit. At this Matsuoka was telling Nomura about "arming ourselves to the teeth for war".

Roosevelt was supplied with MAGIC decrypts by the Army and Navy intelligence units month and month about. But after the problem with the decrypted MAGIC message security was tightened. His military aide, who was nicknamed "Pa" Watson, was the immediate cause. A MAGIC decrypt went missing and after a search it was eventually discovered in his wastepaper basket. The Army refused to let the White House have decrypts for a month. Roosevelt's naval aide was allowed to read them and pass on the information to him. In November Roosevelt insisted on a change in his decrypt delivery system, and his naval aide henceforth supplied all his decrypts. But the MAGIC was still produced on alternate Army and Navy days! [10]

In July Roosevelt, with Churchill's agreement, issued a stern warning to Nomura against further encroachment in South-east Asia which might compel the US to take counter measures even though these might lead to war. Churchill now felt there should be a naval deterrent in the Far East. The Admiralty said no ships were available, but in October it was agreed that the battleship *Prince of Wales* should be sent to join the *Repulse* at Singapore, hoping that they and the US Pacific Fleet in Hawaii would be enough to avert war. General Tojo, who was pro-war, had become Japanese Prime Minister, and although Nomura had still been trying to find some ground for agreement, on 5 November the Japanese Imperial Liaison Conference took the decision to prepare a surprise attack on the US Pacific Fleet at Pearl Harbor on 8 December Tokyo time (7 December, US time).

This was not mentioned at all in any Japanese diplomatic messages, so it did not appear in MAGIC. But a decrypt of a telegram to the Washington Embassy said it was absolutely necessary to settle the dispute with the US not later than 25 November. Next, two telegrams mentioned "immoveable deadlines"; the second moving the deadline to 29 November but saying "that deadline absolutely cannot be changed. After that things are automatically going to happen". [11]

On 25 November Roosevelt, Hull, Stimson and his other advisers discussed what they knew meant war, and where it might start. But apparently an attack on Hawaii did not occur to them. Intelligence was coming in of a Japanese fleet leaving Shanghai, when on 26 November Hull gave Nomura the final terms – Japan was to withdraw from the Tripartite Pact, and give up the occupied territory in China. These terms were obviously unacceptable.

On 27 November, Roosevelt and his advisers believed that the Philippines, Burma or the Burma Road, and the Dutch East Indies were the likely targets. There was no mention of Hawaii, nor was it mentioned in the military intelligence assessment produced that day on the Japanese threat over the next four months. There was no intelligence on the Task Force (which included six aircraft carriers and two battleships) which had left Japan (the Kurile Islands) secretly on 26 November, heading for Pearl Harbor with instructions to deal the US Pacific Fleet "a mortal blow". [12]

Churchill was often in touch with Roosevelt and sent notes on decrypts saying "Make sure the President sees this". On 26 and 28 November, the "Winds Message" was decrypted – sent by Tokyo to its embassies on 19 November. These were coded signals indicating the intention to break off diplomatic relations with Britain, the United States and Russia, and instructing them to destroy all codebooks and machines (for Britain the message was "West wind clear"). [13]

Throughout this period Churchill received decrypts, and Ultra reports under the codename Boniface. Boniface was the fictitious agent to whom all this secret intelligence could be attributed. These documents kept Churchill well-informed on the Japanese diplomatic messages. His constant anxiety was that if Britain had to declare war because Malaya or Singapore were attacked, the US would give immediate armed support. He learned on 2 December that Tokyo had told Oshima in Berlin on 30 November that a breakdown of negotiations was inevitable, and that he should tell Hitler and Ribbentrop that war with Britain and America "may happen sooner than expected"; then notify the Italians. [14]

On 1 December the British War Cabinet and on 3 December the US Defence Committee discussed an imminent threat to Thailand, and it became known that a Japanese force of troop transports, cruisers and destroyers was sailing southwards. On 7 December Britain learned that Roosevelt was prepared to regard as hostile to the US any Japanese attack on Malaya, Burma, the Dutch East Indies or Thailand.

On 7 December Pearl Harbor was attacked. No warning was given because the declaration of war was handed to the Americans after the attack had begun. Over 2,400 people were killed and 18 ships including eight battleships were sunk.

On 8 December Oshima heard of the attack and notified Ribbentrop, who said that immediate participation in the war by Germany and Italy was a matter of course although he had not yet got Hitler's sanction.

Arrangements were made for the joint declaration of war, and agreement of the text of the Three-Power Pact between Germany, Italy and Japan. They would conjointly prosecute the war forced upon them by the US and the British Empire, and would not conclude a separate peace except by mutual consent. One of Oshima's telegrams of 8 December reports that when Ribbentrop received notice of the sinking of the US battleships, he was "greatly delighted and praised highly the daring of our navy". [15]

These telegrams were all decrypted at Bletchley Park and the information forwarded to Churchill in an Ultra report dated 10 December.

Churchill had frequently rung Bletchley Park during the previous few weeks for the latest intelligence. Captain Malcolm Kennedy, one of the leading Japanese cryptanalysts, wrote in his diary on 6 December that Churchill

> "….is all over himself at the moment for latest information and indications re Japan's intentions and rings up at all hours of day and night, except for the 4 hours in each 24 (2 to 6 a.m.) when he sleeps." [16]

Churchill learned of the attack on Pearl Harbor when he put the wireless on at 9.p.m. on 7 December. He immediately rang the White House, and Roosevelt said "They have attacked us at Pearl Harbor. We are all in the same boat now".

PEARL HARBOR : CONCLUSION

Churchill's immense relief that America would now be joining Britain in the war must have been shared by everyone who had any knowledge of our position at that time. From the foregoing account of the decrypts of Japanese diplomatic messages it can be seen that they nowhere mentioned anything to do with Pearl Harbor or Hawaii. Advance notice of the Japanese Fleet's destination was never given to any diplomatic mission. This is generally agreed by those who have had access to all the documents which were supplied to Churchill and to Roosevelt. The various discussions which they held with their advisers in the anxious days before the attack also show that they were not thinking of Pearl Harbor. They considered Malaya, Singapore, Burma, Thailand and the Dutch East Indies, and with justification since all of these were attacked either at the same time as Pearl Harbor or in the weeks following.

But the real argument arises not over the Purple diplomatic messages. It is over whether both the Americans and the British were reading JN 25, the main Japanese fleet code, and whether this gave hints which might have led to Pearl Harbor being considered (or even known) to be the Task Force's objective. Before Pearl Harbor happened there was little in the way of intelligence co-operation except on diplomatic material, e.g. when the PURPLE machine had been delivered to Bletchley Park (and as you remember now, this dealt with the main diplomatic code). It is held by Christopher Andrew, whose book "For the President's Eyes Only" was published in 1995, that the US naval intelligence group Op-20-G had had partial success with JN 25a but when the new version JN 25b was introduced in December 1940 they were unable to read it. From 1939 to 1941 they had usually two and never more than five cryptanalysts to work on all the Japanese naval codes and ciphers, and even in late 1941 their number was only increased to eight. These few people were also working on the alternative month arrangements with the Army's SIS on the PURPLE code, in which there was so much traffic during late 1941.

Yet JN 25b did contain clues. The unsolved messages were decrypted as part of a secret post-war study, and were found to reveal some of the preparations for Pearl Harbor. For example, by mid-November 1941 there were several indications of planning for a surprise attack by a task force including six aircraft carriers on an enemy fleet at anchor somewhere in the North Pacific. The fleet itself maintained radio silence on the long voyage, but weather forecasts for the North Pacific were addressed to the "Strike Force". There was a report on the modification of torpedoes for use in shallow water, which was also indicative since in Washington it was believed that Pearl Harbor was too shallow for a conventional torpedo attack. [17] Frederick D Parker, the historian of the US National Security Agency, is quoted by C Andrew:

> "If the Japanese navy messages had enjoyed a higher priority and [had been] assigned more analytic resources, could the US Navy have predicted the Japanese attack on Pearl Harbor? Most emphatically yes!. [18]

Professor Andrew holds that it was partly due to the low priority that Roosevelt himself gave to naval intelligence, that led to its being so understaffed. The Japanese had maintained a policy of intense secrecy about their forces for several years, so their capabilities were not precisely known and they continued to be underrated even after Pearl Harbor.

Prior to Pearl Harbor, Bletchley Park's Far East Combined Bureau was still at Singapore and would have intercepted the JN 25b messages. They had to remove rapidly to Ceylon on 27 December 1941. Had there been any information they could read bearing on the Pacific situation in the weeks before Pearl Harbor, it is difficult to imagine that it would not have been passed to Churchill and would therefore be in the HW1 archive at the Public Record Office with the Japanese diplomatic messages.

Sir Harry Hinsley, author of the official history of "British Intelligence in the Second World War", told me that as JN 25b was not being read at the time of Pearl Harbor, this information was not available in London. Churchill and the Joint Intelligence Committee knew from the Japanese diplomatic intercepts that a crisis was coming, but not its nature. Hinsley said the problem as to who might have known of Pearl Harbor in advance had arisen because when the US declassified the JN 25b messages which had been decrypted after the war, people did not look at the bottom of the pages and note the dates of decryption. [19]

ATTACK ON CEYLON AND THE BAY OF BENGAL APRIL 1942

This incident was another Pearl Harbor style surprise attack, this time against the Royal Navy Eastern Fleet in Ceylon. It was led by Admiral Nagumo, who had commanded the Pearl Harbor Task Force, and Admiral Ozawa who with his own force raided merchant shipping in the Bay of Bengal. But for reasons which will become obvious, the scale of the attack was not realised until it was nearly over. It is also a fascinating British example of a commander's action being influenced by a known decrypt.

In January 1942 the Admiralty received a report from Chongqing in China of a fleet of 50 Japanese ships with one aircraft carrier sailing south past Taiwan, possibly to attack Ceylon. [20]

On 16 January an Admiralty report considered this information, but did not "place credence" in the idea that this fleet was destined for Ceylon, because the main Japanese fleet was known to be in the south-west Pacific; therefore they concluded that it was probably heading for Burma or Singapore; Ceylon was thought to be no threat to the Japanese, yet its defences would be good enough against a raid, and any attack on them would need air cover. [21]

Force Z, the Royal Navy force sent out to Singapore to join the *Repulse* in November 1941 as a deterrent, consisted of the battleship *Prince of Wales* and four destroyers. The carrier *Indomitable*, which should have joined them, had run aground on a reef in Bermuda. They reached Singapore on 3 December 1941 and sailed five days later with the intention of disrupting the Japanese landings in Malaya. But *Prince of Wales* and *Repulse* were sunk by Japanese air attack on 10 December about 100 miles from Singapore. After this news reached Britain General Sir Alan Brooke, Chief of the Imperial General Staff, wrote in his diary:

> "This means that from Africa eastwards to America, through the Indian Ocean and the Pacific, we have lost control of the sea". [22]

After this disaster, five World War 1 battleships led by the *Warspite* and three aircraft carriers had been hastily sent out to Ceylon to guard the sea approaches to India and the shipping routes to Burma. Two carriers were fast modern ones but the third, *Hermes,* was smaller and older. Along with 8 cruisers, 15 destroyers and 5 submarines these made up the Eastern Fleet, which was divided between Colombo, Trincomalee and a base at Addu Atoll in the Maldives. Admiral Sir James Somerville was recalled from Gibraltar at the end of December to be C-in-C of the Eastern Fleet. He had previously commanded Force H, which had played an important part in sinking the *Bismarck.*

Somerville arrived in Colombo on 28 March 1942. He planned to start training his new forces immediately. But on 29 March he received a most alarming signal.

HMS *Anderson* was the Intelligence Unit of the Eastern Fleet's Headquarters at Colombo, linked to Bletchley Park, and also the home of FECB since its removal from Singapore on 27 December 1941. Here I quote Hugh Denham:

> "They were working one sultry afternoon in Colombo on a message that described plans for a massive attack somewhere. Then they spelt out the name of the place that was to be clobbered – KO-RO-N-BO. An electric shock ran through the up-to-then relaxed office." [23]

This attack was expected on or about 1st April. Admiral Somerville at once ordered all his ships to rendezvous 80 miles south of Ceylon, calculating that the Japanese force's object must be to destroy the British ships and bases in Ceylon. But after three days and nights of searching and sighting nothing, he suspected that the intelligence report might have been wrong. By this time his fleet needed refuelling so he took them to the Addu Atoll base, and sent the carrier *Hermes* with a destroyer to Trincomalee to pick up her planes, and the cruisers *Dorsetshire* and *Cornwall* to Colombo for repairs.

But on 4 April a Catalina pilot sighted three Japanese battleships and an aircraft carrier south of Ceylon. Somerville was 600 miles away and could only try to return as soon as possible. Admiral Nagumo had equally failed to find the British fleet, and assumed that they were in port at Colombo.

The next morning – Easter Sunday – Nagumo's attack began. He had 340 planes to Somerville's 95, and they first shot down the 12 torpedo bombers on their way to join the *Hermes*. But they found the harbour almost empty, so they bombed the port installations and the empty airfield. However 22 of the RAF Hurricanes were lost in the battle against far greater numbers.

The Japanese planes had returned to their carriers when they received a report of two cruisers to the south-west. Hoping this was the Eastern Fleet returning, they launched a second attack. However, it was the *Dorsetshire* and *Cornwall* and they had no chance against the bombers.

Admiral Nagumo then departed eastwards, to avoid fighting at night when his aircraft would be at a disadvantage, whereas Somerville had hoped to attack him at night. After another spell of the fleets' stalking and missing each other, Nagumo went north and attacked Trincomalee on the morning of 7 April. The base had been warned and had cleared the harbour of shipping during the night, so again the Japanese bombers attacked the cranes, fuel storage tanks, and ammunition dumps. Unfortunately the *Hermes* and her destroyer returned too soon, and both were sunk.

Meanwhile in the Bay of Bengal Admiral Ozawa with his cruiser force had attacked a British convoy and sunk 23 merchant ships. As a result all British shipping operations between Burma and India were suspended.

On 9 April both commanders made decisions which ended this incident, without realising what the other was about to do. Admiral Nagumo set sail for Japan, having sunk one British aircraft carrier, two heavy cruisers and a destroyer, and shot down some 32 planes. He had lost no ships, and only a few planes.

After these losses Somerville decided to withdraw the rest of the Eastern Fleet to Mombasa. [24] His evasive action had saved the two modern carriers, Warspite and the elderly "R" class battleships with poorly-armoured decks which would have been sitting ducks against dive bombers. But withdrawal left the Indian Ocean undefended, so that object of the Japanese attack had been achieved. With Nagumo's carrier force and Ozawa's force it was clearly far more than a "raid", but it had lost the element of complete surprise because of the warning given by the KO-RO-N-BO signal. Without that, the result would have been another Pearl Harbor.

From his report to the Admiralty dated 13.4.42, Somerville seems to have been unsure until a late stage what forces Nagumo actually had. He was surprised that the attack on Colombo was carried out in daylight, and until the *Dorsetshire* and *Cornwall* were lost he had not realised that the enemy had a considerable carrier force; nor had he appreciated the fighter dive bomber method of attacking them until the survivors returned. [25] Not until 9 April when the action was over did some Blenheims locate the enemy 200 miles from Trincomalee with four carriers, three battleships, four or five cruisers and two destroyers. [26]

As regards the decision to withdraw to Mombasa, an interesting letter from the Secretary to the First Sea Lord to C-in-C Eastern Fleet, dated 6 April, ends with:

> It is possible that you are finding the presence of the "R" class battleships more of a liability than an asset. Should you consider it desirable to withdraw the "R" class to the West, possibly to Aden or Zanzibar, you have full discretion to do so forthwith. We fully appreciate the very difficult game you are being called upon to play. [27]

Admiral Yamamoto had ordered this campaign in the Indian Ocean to destroy the British fleet.

This is confirmed by a report following information originating with the Japanese Military Attaché in Lisbon, that:

> The Japanese policy is the piecemeal destruction of the British and American fleets, until such time as the Japanese Navy is sufficiently strong to carry out a major action………..a large scale attack is proposed against Ceylon. [28]

THE JAPANESE COURSES

After Pearl Harbor and the declaration of war against Japan, the need for Japanese linguists for military and intelligence work became acute. There were a few specialists in Bletchley Park working with the PURPLE machine on the Japanese diplomatic codes. The Naval Section was working on Japanese naval codes. Outside Bletchley Park there were Japanese specialists in the embassies in the Far East; there were Japanese speakers in businesses there, and teachers and missionaries. But in the lightning advance of the Japanese into Malaya on 7 December, Hong Kong's fall on 25 December, then Singapore on 15 February 1942 and Mandalay on 1 May, large numbers of these people were taken prisoner.

The War Office had been relying on making use of these Japanese speakers in the event of war, but their calculations had gone badly wrong. In Britain the only institution teaching Japanese was SOAS – London University's School of Oriental & African Studies founded in 1917. This was where diplomats studied. But the number of students doing Japanese between 1923 and 1941 averaged only 11 per year.

In the early war years SOAS requested an expansion of language teaching for Japanese and for Middle Eastern and South-East Asian languages. The War Office agreed that courses would be needed in the event of hostilities, but would not agree to funding. In the summer of 1941 the School tried again and approached both the Foreign Office and the War Office. In August the War Office replied:-

> So far as can be reasonably foreseen at present, in spite of the kaleidoscopic changes which have taken place in the countries which might in the future develop into the theatres of war, we feel we are at present reasonably insured in the matter of officers knowing Oriental languages! [29]

Immediately the war started the War Office clamoured for Japanese speakers and SOAS set up a special course for grammar school boys in their last year at school who were studying Classics or German, Russian or French. But SOAS was bombed and the course did not start until May 1942 and was due to end in December 1942. They also ran a 10-week course in Japanese radio signals. [30]

One of the first to foresee the need for Japanese linguists was Brigadier John Tiltman, the head of the Military Section at Bletchley Park. He taught himself enough Japanese to be the main figure in breaking the Japanese military attaché code in summer 1942, so understood the problem. What Bletchley required was a knowledge of written Japanese to deal with Army, Navy and Air Force messages, not the spoken language. He approached SOAS to organise a course to teach undergraduates enough written Japanese to do this in six months. SOAS replied that this took five years in peacetime, and they might be able to do it in two years. However SOAS did run a number of six-month and one-year wartime courses. In July 1942 they started the Services Interrogators' Course, the Services Translators' Course and a Translators' short course, which was how the Forces wanted them arranged. But later these were altered to allow the Interrogator students to learn to read and the Translators to learn conversation, and in June 1944 they became a Services General Purpose Course. Once out in the Far East they had to do whatever was required, and some ex-Bletchley Park people found themselves acting as interrogators of Japanese prisoners. There was always a great demand for Japanese linguists in the Army, especially in Burma, and there were never enough.

The two-year suggestion was far too long to be of use to Bletchley Park. Tiltman then set up the GCCS Japanese course, of which there were eleven up to the end of the war. They were intensive six-month courses, and were taught by Captain Oswald Tuck. Tuck was then 65 and retired from the Royal Navy. He had had a fascinating career, joining the Navy at 15 and serving in the Far East. He studied Japanese by himself, then obtained leave to live in Tokyo and study locally. He passed his interpreter's exams and was eventually appointed assistant to the naval attaché in the British Embassy. During the First World War he worked for naval intelligence and became head of the Admiralty's Historical Section. Before retiring he worked with Arthur Waley, the distinguished Sino-Japanese scholar, censoring Japanese press reports.

The first BP Japanese course started in Bedford on 2 February 1942 in a room above the Gas showrooms, later moved to 52 De Parys Avenue. There were 22 men and one woman, all but three of whom were classical scholars in their first year at Oxford or Cambridge. They had very few teaching aids – a grammar book, a book of printed Japanese characters and three different Japanese-English dictionaries – all belonging to Captain Tuck. [31]

The illustrations will give a feeling of being confronted with Japanese for the first time. A very brief explanation of the different writing systems will help in understanding the problems of learning the language.

The Japanese adopted the Chinese writing system during the seventh and eighth centuries AD when the influence of Buddhism and of Chinese culture was at its height. But Chinese and Japanese are completely different in grammar and construction, so that Chinese characters could not express, for instance, tenses and certain word endings which do not exist in Chinese. The Chinese characters are called Kanji in Japanese, and are used for words borrowed from Chinese, or words which have broadly the same meaning as the Chinese. [32]

Kana consists of two systems, Katakana and Hiragana:-

The symbols of both represent one syllable each (except a.i.u.e.o and n which are single sounds). Any given symbol in Kana always has the same sound value, and each sound can be represented by either a hiragana or a katakana symbol. The vowels can be short or long – a.i.u.e.o.

KATAKANA

ア	イ	ウ	エ	オ
カ	キ	ク	ケ	コ
サ	シ	ス	セ	ソ
タ	チ	ツ	テ	ト
ナ	ニ	ヌ	ネ	ノ
ハ	ヒ	フ	ヘ	ホ
マ	ミ	ム	メ	モ
ヤ	(イ)	ユ	(エ)	ヨ
ラ	リ	ル	レ	ロ
ワ	(イ)	(ウ)	(エ)	ヲ
ン				

キャ	キュ	キョ
シャ	シュ	ショ
チャ	チュ	チョ
ニャ	ニュ	ニョ
ヒャ	ヒュ	ヒョ
ミャ	ミュ	ミョ

リャ	リュ	リョ

ガ	ギ	グ	ゲ	ゴ
ザ	ジ	ズ	ゼ	ゾ
ダ	ヂ	ヅ	デ	ド
バ	ビ	ブ	ベ	ボ
パ	ピ	プ	ペ	ポ

ギャ	ギュ	ギョ
ジャ	ジュ	ジョ

ビャ	ビュ	ビョ
ピャ	ピュ	ピョ

These sheets will give a feeling of being confronted with Japanese for the first time

あ	い	う	え	お
か	き	く	け	こ
さ	し	す	せ	そ
た	ち	つ	て	と
な	に	ぬ	ね	の
は	ひ	ふ	へ	ほ
ま	み	む	め	も
や	(い)	ゆ	(え)	よ
ら	り	る	れ	ろ
わ	(い)	(う)	(え)	を
ん				

きゃ	きゅ	きょ
しゃ	しゅ	しょ
ちゃ	ちゅ	ちょ
にゃ	にゅ	にょ
ひゃ	ひゅ	ひょ
みゃ	みゅ	みょ

りゃ	りゅ	りょ

が	ぎ	ぐ	げ	ご
ざ	じ	ず	ぜ	ぞ
だ	ぢ	づ	で	ど
ば	び	ぶ	べ	ぼ
ぱ	ぴ	ぷ	ぺ	ぽ

ぎゃ	ぎゅ	ぎょ
じゃ	じゅ	じょ

びゃ	びゅ	びょ
ぴゃ	ぴゅ	ぴょ

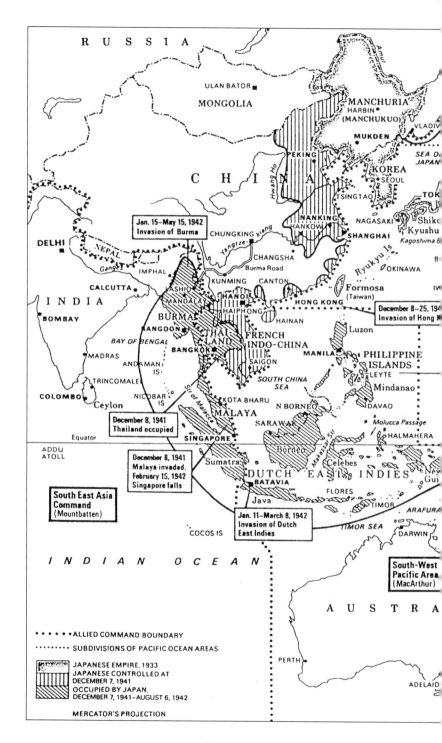

RUSSIA

ULAN BATOR ■
MONGOLIA

MANCHURIA
HARBIN ●
(MANCHUKUO)
VLADIV

MUKDEN ●

PEKING

CHINA

KOREA
SEOUL

TSINGTAO

SEA O
JAPAN

TOK

Shiko
Kyushu
Kagoshima B

Jan. 15–May 15, 1942
Invasion of Burma

CHUNGKING kiang

NANKING
HANKOW

SHANGHAI

NAGASAKI

DELHI ■

NEPAL

Ganges

IMPHAL

Yangtze

CHANGSHA
Burma Road

KUNMING
CANTON

Ryukyu Is
OKINAWA

Formosa
(Taiwan)

IW

B

ASHIO
MANDALAY

HANOI
HAIPHONG

HONG KONG

CALCUTTA ●

INDIA

BURMA

BOMBAY ●

RANGOON ●

BAY OF BENGAL

MADRAS ●

ANDAMAN
IS

TRINCOMALE

THAI-
LAND

FRENCH
INDO-CHINA

BANGKOK

SAIGON

HAINAN

Luzon

MANILA

December 8–25, 194
Invasion of Hong K

PHILIPPINE
ISLANDS

LEYTE

Mindanao

COLOMBO ●

NICOBAR
IS

Ceylon

SOUTH CHINA
SEA

Str of Malacca

KOTA BHARU

N BORNEO

DAVAO

MALAYA

SARAWAK

Molucca Passage

Equator

ADDU
ATOLL

December 8, 1941
Thailand occupied

SINGAPORE ●

Borneo

HALMAHERA

Makassar Str

December 8, 1941
Malaya invaded.
February 15, 1942
Singapore falls

Sumatra

Celebes

DUTCH   EAST   INDIES

Ne
Gui

BATAVIA

FLORES

South East Asia
Command
(Mountbatten)

Java

COCOS IS

Jan. 11–March 8, 1942
Invasion of Dutch
East Indies

TIMOR

ARAFURA

TIMOR SEA

DARWIN

INDIAN   OCEAN

South-West
Pacific Area
(MacArthur)

AUSTRA

PERTH ●

● ● ● ● ●ALLIED COMMAND BOUNDARY

· · · · · · · · SUBDIVISIONS OF PACIFIC OCEAN AREAS

JAPANESE EMPIRE, 1933
JAPANESE CONTROLLED AT
DECEMBER 7, 1941
OCCUPIED BY JAPAN,
DECEMBER 7, 1941–AUGUST 6, 1942

ADELAID

MERCATOR'S PROJECTION

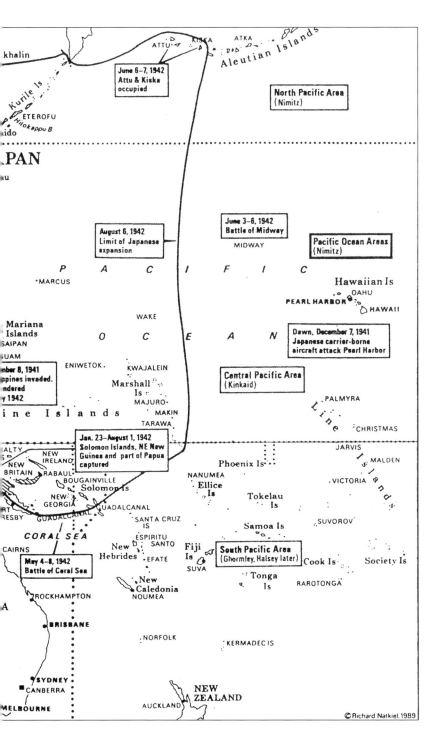

khalin

ATTU KISKA   ATKA
Aleutian Islands

June 6-7, 1942
Attu & Kiska
occupied

North Pacific Area
(Nimitz)

Kurile Is

ETEROFU
Hitokappu B
ido

PAN

August 6, 1942
Limit of Japanese
expansion

June 3-6, 1942
Battle of Midway

MIDWAY

Pacific Ocean Areas
(Nimitz)

P   A   C   I   F   I   C

•MARCUS

Hawaiian Is
• OAHU
PEARL HARBOR•
HAWAII

WAKE

Mariana
Islands
SAIPAN
GUAM

O   C   E   A   N

Dawn, December 7, 1941
Japanese carrier-borne
aircraft attack Pearl Harbor

ENIWETOK•   KWAJALEIN

mber 8, 1941
ppines invaded.
ndered
y 1942

Marshall
Is
MAJURO•

Central Pacific Area
(Kinkaid)

PALMYRA

ine Islands   MAKIN
TARAWA

Line Islands

CHRISTMAS

Jan. 23-August 1, 1942
Solomon Islands, NE New
Guinea and part of Papua
captured

JARVIS
MALDEN

ALTY   NEW
NEW   IRELAND
BRITAIN RABAUL
BOUGAINVILLE
NEW   Solomon Is
GEORGIA
RT   GUADALCANAL
RESBY GUADALCANAL•

Phoenix Is•

NANUMEA
•Ellice
Is

•VICTORIA

Tokelau
Is

SANTA CRUZ
IS

Samoa Is

SUVOROV

CORAL SEA

CAIRNS

ESPIRITU
New b SANTO
Hebrides •EFATE

Fiji
Is
SUVA

South Pacific Area
(Ghormley, Halsey later)

Cook Is

Society Is

May 4-8, 1942
Battle of Coral Sea

•New
Caledonia
NOUMEA

Tonga
Is

RAROTONGA

ROCKHAMPTON

A

BRISBANE

•NORFOLK

•KERMADEC IS

SYDNEY
CANBERRA

MELBOURNE

AUCKLAND

NEW
ZEALAND

© Richard Natkiel. 1989

勘 729	勺 740	旬 747	旨 752	匹 756	巨 758	匠 761	匡 764	克 772	裁 781
紊 782	乾 784	裁 788	載 789	占 799	卓 802	貞 803	却 808	卸 812	灰 820
厘 823	暦 833	忘 851	又 855	双 859	叔 861	叙 862	桑 864	叫 881	吐 883
吸 885	呈 895	吟 898	吹 901	呼 914	咲 922	唆 925	哲 931	啓 940	唯 942
喚 958	喫 961	嗣 969	嘆 974	嘱 989	噴 995	嚇 1008	囚 1024	困 1033	圏 1045
吉 1053	坊 1062	坑 1063	坪 1072	城 1078	埋 1084	域 1085	培 1091	堕 1092	堅 1096
執 1097	堤 1108	塔 1109	塔 1112	塑 1121	塊 1122	塗 1124	墜 1132	墳 1141	墾 1142
壇 1146	壊 1147	壁 1148	奔 1175	奇 1176	契 1177	奏 1178	奨 1181	奪 1183	奴 1186
妃 1188	如 1189	好 1191	妨 1196	妊 1197	妙 1199	姓 1203	姻 1214	姿 1215	姫 1216
娠 1220	娘 1225	娯 1226	婆 1234	婚 1236	婿 1239	媒 1241	嫁 1249	嫡 1253	嬢 1257
孔 1265	孤 1270	宅 1279	宇 1280	宜 1290	宙 1291	宝 1293	宰 1303	宴 1304	寂 1315
密 1316	寛 1325	寝 1326	寧 1335	寡 1337	寶 1339	寮 1340	審 1341	寸 1348	封 1349
肖 1360	掌 1366	輝 1371	尺 1377	尼 1378	尽 1380	尿 1382	尾 1383	屈 1386	層 1402
履 1404	岐 1410	峠 1416	峡 1417	峰 1423	崇 1429	崩 1430	巧 1453	攻 1457	貢 1458
項 1459	忌 1463	巻 1466	帆 1469	帽 1483	幅 1484	幣 1490	干 1492	幻 1494	幼 1495
幾 1496	庁 1498	床 1503	座 1515	唐 1516	廊 1519	庸 1520	庶 1522	廃 1526	廉 1530
腐 1532	慶 1539	廷 1546	弊 1551	弓 1560	弧 1567	弦 1568	弾 1575	尋 1585	彩 1590
彰 1593	影 1594	径 1602	征 1603	彼 1604	徐 1612	循 1625	街 1626	御 1628	微 1631
徴 1634	徹 1637	衝 1638	衡 1641	忙 1647	忍 1648	怖 1662	怒 1664	怪 1665	恨 1677
恭 1680	恵 1681	悔 1682	恒 1683	恐 1685	悦 1696	患 1697	悩 1698	悟 1700	悼 1706
惑 1710	惜 1712	惨 1713	慌 1725	愉 1726	惰 1727	愁 1729	愚 1730	慨 1741	慎 1742
慢 1755	憎 1757	慰 1758	憩 1765	憤 1773	憾 1778	憶 1780	懇 1781	懐 1782	懲 1785

Chinese ideograms, called Kanji in Japanese, were given numbers which were then enciphered.

Kana Morse was used for transmitting Japanese messages. Each kana syllable had a Morse sign, as did the ten numbers. British wireless operators who intercepted Japanese messages were vital to the codebreaking operation, and had to be trained in Kana Morse. [33]

Because they are phonetic, kana are very useful for incorporating foreign words into Japanese. There are a great many, like "arubeito" meaning "part-time work" but taken from the German word for work "arbeit". Katakana is used for these foreign words e.g. "metoro netowaku" = metro network. Hiragana is used for word endings; grammatical particles (postpositions) e.g. "from" which follows the word, and some Japanese words that do not have kanji. It might seem easier to do away with kanji altogether, as it is possible to write entirely in kana; or even to use Romaji – the romanized script. But this is no easy solution because Japanese suffers from "sound poverty" i.e. has very few sounds, so there are vast numbers of kanji to each sound, all with different meanings. Therefore if you write it all out in romaji (i.e the syllables in our alphabet) there will be great ambiguity as to the meaning. At least if you have the kanji/characters, which all look different even though they may have the same sound, you will arrive at the meaning!

The most useful attribute for learning characters is a good and preferably a photographic memory.

The students on the Bedford courses used the flash-card method – characters with their meanings and pronunciations had to be written out on cards and memorized. By the end of six months they had learnt some 1200 characters. In our Archives here we have a set of their flash-cards. This system is still used as part of learning Chinese and Japanese. The vocabulary was that needed for translating the formal military, naval and air force signals and captured documents (likely to be reports, requests or orders) and they did not learn anything else – not the conversation for a polite tea party.

A similar course was run in 1943 inside Bletchley Park, with students chosen from people already working there. The teacher was John Lloyd, one of a group of consular officers who knew Japanese and who had joined the Park staff. My informant had been a Wren, living and working at Woburn for two years, before taking this course. Afterwards she was set to work in the Library on captured documents – all naval material, including maps, charts and sailors' diaries. [34]

At the end of these courses the students went on a month's codebreaking exercise. Tiltman always called on the students on each course to see how they were getting on. Then they were assigned to their places of work. Of the writers of chapters on Far East codebreaking in "Codebreakers", Michael Loewe, Maurice Wiles and Hugh Denham were on the first course, and were sent to Bletchley Park where the majority of Bedford students found themselves at first, although some were later transferred to intelligence units abroad linked to the Park such as Delhi or Colombo. Michael Loewe joined the Naval Section, first at Elmers (a large Victorian house on the left of the parish church, which had been a school. [35] It was mysteriously burnt down one Guy Fawkes Night about 1980 and there are now houses on the site). Later he was in Hut 7 and in B Block beyond the lake. Building went on all through the war in the Park, as the volume of work and the numbers of staff increased, so the original Huts all had parts of their staff working in other buildings. The Naval Section worked on Japanese merchant and naval codes, such as JN 11 – a four figure merchant code, and JN 25 – the main naval code used by all ships including submarines, the four major Japanese naval bases and shore stations around the Pacific. JN 25 was a five figure code, and was the one which, as we have seen, caused so much speculation as to whether it gave some warning of Pearl Harbor.

JAPANESE CODE SYSTEMS

The Japanese, unlike the Germans, used many totally different codes and ciphers, probably 55 in all during the course of the war. They were mostly based on numerals rather than on letters. Letter-codes were reserved for lower-grade signals. Because the Pacific is such an enormous area the Japanese experienced difficulties in sending out new keys or codebooks over the huge distances to replace current ones, thus aiding the Allies where they had already broken the current codes. Perhaps the most famous example of this is the Battle of Midway, where the JN 25b replacement (to be JN 25c) codebook distribution was due on 1 April 1942, but was postponed first to 1 May and then to 1 June. By then the Americans had discovered not only the plans for what was to be a surprise Japanese attack on the Midway base, but almost at the last moment the date, 3 June.

On 1 June the code changed and the American naval cryptanalysts could not read it. But they already had all the information needed to deliver the surprise attack themselves, and gain their first naval victory in the Pacific, at Midway.

In April 1943 JN 25 enabled the Americans to shoot down Admiral Yamamoto's plane in the Solomon Islands and it gave the warning of the Japanese attack on Ceylon.

JN 36 and 37 were meteorological codes read at Bletchley,

JN 40, broken at Kilindini in November 1942, was a merchant shipping code used to report attacks on Allied submarines or aircraft. The user wrote the message out in kana syllables and substituted two digits for each syllable. This often revealed the detailed routes of convoys and identity of some of the ships.

A few were book codes, i.e. both sender and recipient possess copies of the same novel or other literary work, and quote pages and numbers to refer to letters or words which spell out the message. Alan Stripp, from whose most informative book "Codebreaker in the Far East" these examples are taken, refers to one book code as having used the Authorised Version of the Bible in English!. [36]

Morse	Basic	"Nigori	o Hanagori	ENGLISH
— · · ·	HA ハ	DA バ	PA パ	B
·	HE ヘ	BE ベ	PE ペ	E
— — · · —	HI ヒ	DI ビ	PI ピ	
— · ·	HO ホ	BO ボ	PO ポ	D
— — · ·	FU フ	BU ブ	PU プ	Z
· — · ·	KA カ	GA ガ		L.
— · — —	KE ケ	GE ゲ		Y
— · — · ·	KI キ	GI ギ		
— — — —	KO コ	GO ゴ		
· · · —	KU ク	GU グ		V
— · · —	MA マ			X
— · · · —	ME メ			
· · — · —	MI ミ			
— · · — ·	MO モ			
—	MU ム			T
· — ·	NA ナ			
— — · —	NE ネ			
— · — ·	NI ニ			
· · — —	NO ノ			
· · · ·	NU ヌ			
· · ·	RA ラ			
— — —	RE レ			
— — ·	RI リ			
· — · —	RO ロ			
— · — — ·	RU ル			
— · — · —	SA サ	ZA ザ		
· — — — ·	SE セ	ZE ゼ		
— — · — ·	SI シ	ZI ジ		
— — — ·	SO ソ	ZO ゾ		
— — — · —	SU ス	ZU ズ		
— ·	TA タ	DA ダ		N
· — · — ·	TE テ	DE デ		
· · — ·	TI チ	DI ヂ		F
· · — · ·	TO ト	DO ド		
· — — ·	TU ツ	DU ヅ		P
— · —	WA ワ			K
· — — · ·	WE ヱ			
· — · · —	WI ヰ			
· — — —	WO ヲ			J
· — —	YA ヤ			W
— —	YO ヨ			M
— · · — —	YU ユ			
— — · — —	A ア			
— · — — —	E エ			
· —	I イ			A
· — · · ·	O オ			
· · —	U ウ			U
· — · — ·	N ン			
· · — — · ·	?			I

· — — — —		1
· · — — —		2
· · · — —		3
· · · · —		4
· · · · ·		5
— · · · ·		6
— — · · ·		7
— — — · ·		8
— — — — ·		9
— — — — —		0

Numerals

PROCEDURE

T	E"YA	Send V's
R	A"KA	Call identification
Q	O"NO	Will call again at...
	KAN	Signal strength 1-5
	KON	Station interference
H	SATU	Atmosph. interference
S	MUFU	Have no traffic
O	YUFU	Have traffic
G	BAKA	Operator reprimand
	SARA	Urgent
	KURE	Go ahead
	KIN	Urgent priority
	SAN	Priority
	UNA	Routine
	YOTU	I am calling ...
	YOFU	You are being called
N		by...
F	HA HA HA	Air raid
	KUHA KUHA KUHA	Air raid
P		time
K	KUKA KUKA KUKA	All clear

Morse	
· — · · — · ·	English to follow
— · · — — · —	Romaji to follow
· — · · — · ·	BT numbers to follow
· — — · —	Long sound
— · — — · —	( )

The Kana Morse system differs from the usual method. From a wartime manual.

JAPANESE MILITARY ATTACHÉ CODES

JMA, the Military Attaché code already mentioned, was broken at Bletchley Park in summer 1942. Maurice Wiles, who was on the first Bedford course, was sent to help Tiltman with breaking this. He describes JMA as a two-letter code in which the kana syllables stood for themselves, and other two-letter groups stood for common words and phrases. (All these were written out in a complicated pattern inside a grid.) But many words had to be spelt out in full in kana, as were foreign names e.g. CHI-YA-A-CHI-RU. (Churchill). This helped in decoding, as did the encoding of numbers as patterned groups e.g. AK = 1, BL = 2, CM = 4. JMA continued to be read throughout the war with only a few short gaps. [37]

There is a box of JMA index cards in the Archives, which show what varied information the Japanese Military Attachés dealt with. There are cards on enemy personnel and units, armaments of every kind, and regular reports on the current situation in numerous countries.

Many relate to the manufacture and purchase of chemicals and metals e.g.

> One Chemical Products and Metals Section deals with steel; shells; cartridge case manufacture; detonators; and synthetic oil and products; German synthetic petrol; producing liquid fuel from coal, and even "German interest in Japanese production of petrol from fir-tree roots".
> Under "War Reports – Personnel: German:" there are inquiries about and proposals for sending German technicians to Japan.
> Under "Chemicals – Purchase of":- (all between Tokyo and Berlin)
> Spanish mercury; ethyl dibromide; neon gas, lubricating oil, formic acid, ethylene and asbestos.

Among these are three very interesting entries, and three more from a section on "Intelligence – Information Requests": all in 1943:

Substitution of STRONTIUM ore for STRONTIUM salt	Tokyo/Berlin, 6 March '43
Asks for main formulae for the Strontium Nitrate.	
Is to be purchased from Germany	Berlin/Tokyo, 26 May '43
Enquiries about pitchblend (sic)	Berlin/Tokyo, 1 September '43
Asks for reply to queries about pitch-blend: Berlin/Tokyo,	22 September '43
Asks for uranium oxide and pitchblende	Tokyo/Berlin, 14 November '43
Details of purchases of pitchblende & zansai Berlin/Tokyo,	20 November '43

Pitchblende is a uranium ore. It is difficult not to believe that these references to strontium and pitchblende, and purchasing them from Germany, mean that Japan was engaged in nuclear research. I have so far not been able to find any mention of this in the document. [38]

However it is known that at least three U-boats set forth for Japan with large quantities of lead. [39] Of these U860 did not get there; it was carrying 104 tons of lead. U861 with 110 tons of lead reached Japan safely. U234 was the third, with 67 tons of lead.
A codebreaker of irreproachable standing informed the Trust that he knew a U-boat with

a serial number set sail for Japan and surrendered at Portsmouth, New Hampshire, at the end of the war. He told us that U-234's cargo included 1232 lbs. of uranium: it is to be inferred that the lead was shielding for the radio-active material. The cargo manifest, which is in our Japanese Exhibition, is consistent with this information. On board U234 were a German general and a dozen technicians, and two Japanese commanders who refused to surrender, above all to the Americans, so had to be allowed to commit suicide and were buried at sea. (We went to Portsmouth, New Hampshire, in September 1996 and talked to a lady in the museum there. She remembered two U-boats being in the harbour at that time, though of course she did not know what their cargoes were).

Another Bletchley Park section dealt with JAAF – Japanese Army Air Force codes. Alan Stripp, who was on the second Bedford course, was assigned to this section and spent 6 months in 1944 working with some 20 others in a room in F Block on JAAF code 6633. They translated messages which had already been decoded. 6633 carried a great deal of information, mostly from Burma, on air units, their movements, Allied attacks on Japanese aircraft and airfields, reports on fuel and ammunition stocks etc. There were other groups in other rooms working on different JAAF codes, but like everyone else at Bletchley Park they had very little contact with anyone in different sections. [40]

THE INTERCEPT STATIONS

The only pre-war British intercept unit in the Far East concerned with Japanese signal and other intelligence was the Far East Combined Bureau, which was set up in Hong Kong in 1934, as an outpost of GCCS. From 1937 it had a small Australian contingent. In 1940 the Australian General Staff established its own signals intelligence unit. They had intercept stations at Melbourne, Canberra, Brisbane and Darwin, and co-operated with FECB in Hong Kong and the Dutch in Java (but when the Japanese invaded Java the staff went to Darwin and Arlington, Virginia).

In 1939 FECB was moved from Hong Kong to Singapore, where it remained until just after Pearl Harbor. On 27 December 1941 it moved again, to Ceylon. Arlington was the US equivalent of Bletchley Park, both the Royal Canadian Navy station at Ottawa and two units on the West Coast of the USA were part of the network. In India, Bletchley Park had a large outstation called the Wireless Experimental Centre in Delhi. WEC with its two outstations: Western Wireless Sub-Centre at Bangalore in S India, and Eastern Wireless Sub-Centre at Barrackpore near Calcutta, dealt mainly with the Japanese forces traffic from Burma. There was also a large US signals intelligence unit in Delhi. HMS *Anderson* in Colombo and Kilindini near Mombasa were naval intelligence units. Even the Ceylon unit had to move when Colombo was attacked, and from April 1942 to August 1943 was at Kilindini, then returned to Colombo.

The problem with Far Eastern traffic was the enormous distances it had to travel. In the UK the only intercept station that could pick up Japanese signals was Flowerdown near Winchester, and then it was only possible for some three hours a day. This was why the Colombo and Kilindini stations were set up. Most of the Japanese signals worked on in Bletchley Park had been intercepted by one of the overseas stations and sent to Bletchley encoded by Type-X machine or one-time pad, in case it might be intercepted by the Japanese and recognised as their own. However a good part of the traffic was sent without risk by submarine cable to South Africa, and then to Britain. [41]

One small puzzle concerns interception. In 1945 Mr Ken Fuller of Bletchley, on board HMS *Montclare,* arrived in Manus in the Admiralty Islands about 1000 miles north of Darwin. *Montclare* spent some time in Manus, then set off alone into the Pacific and anchored at various islands, where she intercepted and apparently re-transmitted signals. They gradually moved north as the US and Australian forces conquered more of the Pacific islands. On board were people who could encode and decode, but no one really knew much about what they were doing, although they were closely linked with the Americans. If anyone can throw any light on the activities of the *Montclare* or any other similar ship, please let me know. (Incidentally while at Manus and further north a small Japanese plane attacked them several times, and they eventually discovered that it came from a submarine). [42]

The Japanese naval section at Bletchley Park exchanged information with its naval counterpart in Washington, OP-20-G. Those working on the Japanese Army and Air Force did likewise with the US Army and apparently felt considerable rivalry – "to solve them and tell Washington first was a great incentive". This arrangement meant that valuable time was not wasted when one side had not found a solution. [43]

In June 1942, as part of the US/British intelligence co-operation, one US Army Special Branch cryptanalyst and two from Op-20-G started work at Bletchley Park. They were the first of many American cryptanalysts and linguists to join various sections. But full co-operation was established in Spring 1943, when Harry Hinsley (then only 23) was sent to Washington by Bletchley Park to conduct negotiations first with Op-20-G on the exchange of all U-boat signals intercepted on either side of the Atlantic; a similar exchange applied to the Far East. He then went on to negotiate the BRUSA Agreement with the US Army Special Branch, the second clause of which stated: "The US will assume as a main responsibility the reading of Japanese Military and Air Codes and ciphers." But he had to contend with the rivalry of the two US intelligence services – he could not tell the Navy (Op-20-G) any details of the BRUSA Agreement because it was with the Army!. [44]

This was the basis of intelligence co-operation until the end of the war.

Organisation of BRUSA arrangements for collaboration between the Allies.

NOTES:

1. "BRUSA" - Circuit using C.C.M.

2. "35C" - Using ECM (Later changed to "34C", using C.C.M.)

3. R.A.F. O.T.P. and U.S. Weather Bureau O.T.P. are essentially similar, using 5-fig. groups.

4. Naval "ULTRA" Pad used in E. Indies Station was 4-fig. Pad. (Later 4-fig. Pad used for Anderson Broadcast to Y parties.)

ULTRA/ZIP/F.455

ŌSHIMA HIROSHI: JAPANESE AMBASSADOR TO BERLIN

Ōshima, the Japanese Ambassador to Berlin during the war, had started his career there as Military Attaché in 1934, and became Ambassador in 1938. This position meant that he was at the centre of the Axis, and thus the intermediary through whom information passed between Tokyo and Berlin, particularly after Japan entered the war. The codes that he and his military and naval attachés used were read by Bletchley Park during most of the war, and produced most valuable information on German policy and actions, as at the time of Pearl Harbor. He predicted Hitler's attack on Russia, and gave many details on new armaments such as the U-boats which were sent to the Indian Ocean in 1942-3, and of the German plans for destroying London and indeed Britain with V-weapons.

In October 1943 he made a famous report on his tour of the Atlantic Wall defences, from Brest southwards, which shows how detailed his information often was. This report was encrypted in 34 separate telegrams and sent by radio to Japan. All were intercepted and later decrypted, at Bletchley Park. He gave the names of the commanders of the various areas, how their armies were organised and how many divisions each had. He described the fortifications, which were not continuous but were a series of independent strong points, with gaps closed by landmines. These strong points all had up-to-date armaments, and three weeks' food supply. There was a large mobile reserve with infantry, Panzer and motorised divisions. The defences of Brest, Lorient, St Nazaire, La Rochelle and Bordeaux had been strengthened, and – familiar to anyone who has visited the Channel Islands – "reinforced concrete used without stint". The coastal defences, he says, are all very close to the beach, so the German plan is to destroy Allied landing operations at the water's edge. He also states that the Germans attach importance to the different sectors as follows:-

a)   the Straits
b)   Normandy and the Brittany peninsula
c)   the Atlantic coast and South of France are regarded as secondary [45]

So in October 1943, six months before D-Day, the British authorities knew that the Germans regarded the Straits as the most important sector, rather than Normandy, and how the defences were organised in the Atlantic area.

The next examples of similar information come from the Japanese Ambassador to Vichy France in April 1944. This particular file illustrates perfectly how such information went from Bletchley Park to Churchill, and further. On 3 April Churchill requested any Boniface telegrams of the last fortnight referring to divisions of the German defence force on the Riviera coast and near Lyons. On 4 April he received a letter from 'C' (Sir Stewart Menzies, head of the Secret Intelligence Services, who always gave Churchill his decrypts). 'C' writes

> I attach the Boniface message which you wish to see again, together with the Chief of the Imperial General Staff's observations thereon. I also submit a BJ Report (130033), received today, from the Japanese Ambassador, Vichy, which deals with German defences in the South of France.

Underneath is written in red ink

C. Send this to General Eisenhower with my compliments and kindly R (report) to me. WSC.

Beneath that is a note in green ink.

Prime Minister. Seen by General Eisenhower 4.4.44. C 6.4.44

The Boniface telegram is marked "From: Duty Officer Hut 3" at Bletchley Park, and is a compilation from several reports from the Japanese Military Attaché at Vichy to Tokyo. It states that the primary object of German defences in Holland, Belgium and France is to 'hold firmly on to the coast' and destroy the Allies on the sea and on the beaches, or as near the coast as possible. Movement of mobile reserves and remarks on roads follow (17 February).

Then comes information on four infantry and two armoured divisions sent in March as reinforcements to Avignon, Montpellier, Toulouse and Bordeaux (26 Feb). Lastly, command of the three armies in Holland, Belgium and N France where they expect the Allied landings, is to be transferred from Rundstedt to Rommel. The CIGS report dated 29 March confirms that the movement of German divisions, and the higher command details given by the Military Attaché are correct.

The Japanese Ambassador to Vichy's latest report dated 1st April 1944 is of a tour he has just made to the defence installations in the South of France. Hitherto there have been three divisions each in the east and west of the region, but the west is to have an extra division. Concrete tank barriers have been erected all along the coast where possible, and old French fortifications as at Toulon and Marseilles have been strengthened, and new ones built at any possible landing points such as Nice, San Rafael, and in the west Sète and Agde. A total of over eight divisions and "numberless" land and sea mines, in short "spectacular progress" has been made since September 1943. [46]

Meanwhile between 20 – 24 April 1944 Õshima's naval attaché was conducted round the German military defences in Northern France by the German Navy. His detailed report to Tokyo was again decoded at Bletchley Park. He inspected some 300 kms. of the coast between Le Havre and Ostend, where there was a total of 52 naval batteries. He describes the various guns at the harbours of Calais, Le Havre and Ostend, and many other batteries installed in bunkers along areas of the coast considered to be at high risk of landings. These are equipped with radar "of a 1940 type". Mines and landmines have been laid, and obstructions made with ferro-concrete piles against landing craft. There are flame-throwers, depth charge throwers, anti-submarine nets, and anti-tank guns installed; even the dimensions of anti-tank ditches (depth 3m and width 20m) is stated!

He then gives his observations – that the enemy's chance of success is slight, despite his command of the sea and air superiority, because the German defences have been planned with precision and executed with thoroughness. He agrees with the German estimate that the main invasion force will land between Ostend and Boulogne, with possible diversions in the Le Havre-Cherbourg area. This again confirms that the Deception Campaign was working well, because the Germans are still not expecting the main invasion in Normandy. However he is very accurate in estimating that the attack will happen during the first ten days of June. Finally – this is ironic – he considers that in the matter of intelligence the Allies are superior to the Germans, because their

> intelligence network is spread throughout France with many ramifications.........the enemy is to a certain extent informed of defence policy, of the actual state of the defences, and of the result of air attack etc. in areas such as northern and southern France. [47]

These decrypted documents illustrate the importance of breaking codes in depth – that understanding Japanese codes cast light not only on their own plans but also so much on those of the Germans. They are examples of the outstanding work done at Bletchley Park.

It took time to learn to use signals intelligence effectively. The understanding of the Japanese codes never quite reached the systematic penetration of the German ciphers. However, the breaking of Japanese ciphers contributed to matters as diverse as the failure of the Pearl Harbor type of operation at Colombo, to the understanding of the German defences of the West, and even perhaps to the decision to drop the atomic bombs on Japan.

NOTES

Events and Negotiations leading up to Pearl Harbor

1. Map "Growth of Japan's Empire", Edwin O. Reischauer & Albert M. Craig, "Japan: Tradition and Transformation", Allen & Unwin, Sydney, 1979, p. 235.

2. Map "The Sea War in the Pacific Hemisphere", ed. Stephen Howarth, "Men of War", London, Weidenfeld & Nicolson, 1992.

3. Robin Denniston, "Churchill's Secret War" Sutton Publishing Ltd., Stroud, 1997, Ch. 2, p. 23.

4. Christopher Andrew, "For the President's Eyes Only", Harper Collins, London 1995, Ch. 2, p. 105.

5. 5. Ibid, p. 106.

6. D. Kahn, "The Codebreakers" p.266. Sphere Books 1980.

7. R. Denniston, op.cit., Ch. 1, pp. 8-9, and note 18, p. 172.

British/US Co-operation before Pearl Harbor

8. C. Andrew, "For the President's Eyes Only", p. 107.

9. For a detailed account of the *Automedon* incident see James Rusbridger and Eric Nave, "Betrayal at Pearl Harbor", Michael O'Mara Books, London 1992, Ch. 5, pp. 96-106.

10. C. Andrew op. Cit. P. 111.

11. Ibid., p. 111

12. Ibid., p. 113

13. Ibid., p. 113

14. HW1/288. Foreign Minister, Tokyo to Japanese Ambassador, Berlin, 30 Nov. 1941. (BJ/85)

15. HW1/313. Japanese Ambassador, Berlin to Foreign Minister, Tokyo, 8 Dec. 1941. (BJ/96)
These telegrams were all decoded at Bletchley Park and the information sent to Churchill, the Foreign Office, War Office, Admiralty and Air Ministry. BJ/96 is a long report on a number of telegrams.

16. John Ferris, "From Broadway House to Bletchley Park: the Diary of Captain Malcolm Kennedy, 1934-1946", Intelligence and National Security, vol. 4 (1989), no. 3. Quoted by C. Andrew, op. Cit., p. 121.

Pearl Harbor: Conclusion

17. C. Andrew, op. Cit. Pp. 120-121.

18. Frederick D. Parker, "The Unsolved Messages of Pearl Harbor", Cryptologia, Vol. 15. (1991), no. 4, quoted by C. Andrew, op. Cit.

19. Sir Harry Hinsley, telephone conversation, 25 February 1997.

Attack on Ceylon and Bay of Bengal April 1942

20. WO 208/924, Jan. 1942, report to Admiralty from Chongqing, China.

21. Ibid., 16 Jan. 1942, Admiralty report.

22. Sir Alan Brooke, CIGS, quoted by John Costello, "The Pacific War" Collins, USA 1982, p. 159.

23. Hugh Denham, "Codebreakers" ed. F.H. Hinsley & A. Stripp, OUP 1993, Ch. 27, p. 275.

24. Most accounts of this attack are extremely short. The most interesting and detailed account is given in J. Costello, "The Pacific War", pp. 229-232.

25. ADM223/259, C-in-C, Eastern Fleet to Admiralty, 13 April 1942.

26. Ibid, 10 April 1942.

27. ADM 223/259, Secretary to First Sea Lord to C-in-C Eastern Fleet, 6 April 1942.

28. Kiyoshi Ikeda on Admiral Chuichi Nagumo in "Men of War" (ed. Howarth) p. 266. WO 208/924, Combined Intelligence Report No. 21, No. 6 JAPAN, 21 April 1942.

The Japanese Courses

29. Sadao Oba, "The 'Japanese' War", Tokyo 1988; Japan Library/Curzon Press 1995, translated by Anne Kaneko, p. 6.

30. Ibid., pp. 8-9. The SOAS courses lasted five years and taught 640 people, p. 140.

31. Alan Stripp, "Codebreaker in the Far East", OUP 1989, Ch. 13, pp. 139-142.

32. Hilary A. Jarvis for notes on Japanese language, and illustrations of kanji, katakana and hiragana.

33. Hugh Skillen, "Spies of the Airwaves", Great Britain 1989, Appendix 2, Japanese Kana Morse.

34. Mrs. Kitty Wyatt, personal communication, 6 October 1996. M. Loewe, "Codebreakers", Ch. 26, p. 262.

35. M. Loewe, op. Cit., p. 259-60.

36. A. Stripp, "Codebreakers", Ch. 7, pp. 65-72.

37. M. Wiles, "Codebreakers", Ch. 28, pp. 283-4.

38. Bletchley Park Trust Archives: Japanese Military Attaché reference cards, box 108.

39. Ibid.: Cargoes carried from Germany to Japan.

40. A. Stripp, "Codebreaker in the Far East", Ch. 2, p. 21.

41. Ibid., Ch. 10, pp.93-98.

42. K. J. Fuller, HMS *Montclare* in Pacific Feb-Nov. 1945. Personal communication. J. Costello, "The Pacific War", p. 455.

43. M. Wiles, "Codebreakers". Ch. 29, p. 285.

44. C. Andrew, op. Cit., Ch. 3, pp. 136-7.
BRUSA Network diagram, Bletchley Park Trust Archives.

Ōshima: Japanese Ambassador to Berlin

45. M.I. 14 Appreciations 6/9/43 – 27/12/43, WO 208/4311, quoted in H. Hinsley, "British Intelligence int he Second World War" Vol. 3, Part 2, Appendix 5, p. 771.

46. HW1/2686 contains all the documents mentioned, which were sent to Churchill in response to his request.

47. HW1/2768.

BIBLIOGRAPHY

Andrew C:	For the President's Eyes Only. Harper Collins 1995.
Bennett R:	Intelligence Investigations – how Ultra changed History. Frank Cass 1996.
Calvocoressi et al:	Total War. 2d Edn. Penguin 1989.
Costello J:	The Pacific War. Collins 1981.
Denniston R:	Churchill's Secret War. Sutton 1997.
Edwards B:	Salvo! Classic Naval Gun Actions. Cassell 1995.
Gilbert M:	Winston S Churchill, Vol VI Finest Hour 1939. Heinemann 1983.
Hinsley H & Stripp A. eds:	Codebreakers. OUP 1993.
Howarth S. ed:	Men of War – Great Naval Leaders of WWII. Weidenfeld & Nicholson 1992.
Howarth S.:	Morning Glory. The Japanese Imperial Navy. Hamish Hamilton 1983.
Kahn D:	The Codebreakers. Weidenfeld & Nicholson 1973.
Lewin R:	Ultra goes to War. 1978.
Sadao Oba:	The 'Japanese' War. Tokyo 1988 trans. Kaneko A. Japan Library/Curzon Press 1995.
Reischauer & Craig: 1979.	Japan – Tradition & Transformation. Allen & Unwin
Rusbridger J & Nave E:	Betrayal at Pearl Harbor. O'Mara 1991.
Skillen H:	Spies of the Airwaves. Privately published 1989.
Stripp A:	Codebreaker in the Far East. OUP 1989.